Major US Historical Wars

War in Afghanistan
Overthrow of the Taliban and Aftermath

Dorothy Kavanaugh

Mason Crest
Philadelphia

Mason Crest
450 Parkway Drive, Suite D
Broomall, PA 19008
www.masoncrest.com

Printed and bound in the United States of America.

CPSIA Compliance Information: Batch #MUW2015. For further information, contact Mason Crest at 1-866-MCP-Book.

3 5 7 9 8 6 4 2

Library of Congress Cataloging-in-Publication Data

ISBN: 978-1-4222-3360-3 (hc)
ISBN: 978-1-4222-8600-5 (ebook)

Major US Historical Wars series ISBN: 978-1-4222-3352-8

About the Author: Dorothy Kavanaugh is a writer and editor who lives near Philadelphia. Her books include *Infamous Terrorists* (Eldorado Ink, 2013) and *The Muslim World: An Overview* (Mason Crest, 2009).

Picture Credits: Federal Bureau of Investigation: 30; Library of Congress: 33, 42; National Archives: 19, 20, 21; North Atlantic Treaty Organization photo: 50, 51, 53, 54 (top), 55, 56; OTTN Publishing: 15; 360b / Shutterstock.com: 40; Larry Bruce / Shutterstock.com: 7; Northfoto / Shutterstock.com: 23, 25, 26; Ken Tannenbaum / Shutterstock.com: 9; Pal Teravagimov / Shutterstock.com: 28; United Nations: 16, 17, 24, 29, 54 (bottom); U.S. Army photo: 1, 31, 36, 37, 43, 47; U.S. Department of Defense: 11, 13, 35, 38, 39, 41, 44, 45, 46, 48, 49, 52; U.S. Navy photo: 10.

Table of Contents

Introduction   5
1: The Attack on America   7
2: A Country in Turmoil   13
3: Civil War in Afghanistan   23
4: Bringing Down the Taliban   33
5: Resurgence of the Taliban   45

Chronology   58
Further Reading / Internet Resources   61
Index   62
Series Glossary   64

KEY ICONS TO LOOK FOR:

Words to Understand: These words with their easy-to-understand definitions will increase the reader's understanding of the text, while building vocabulary skills.

Sidebars: This boxed material within the main text allows readers to build knowledge, gain insights, explore possibilities, and broaden their perspectives by weaving together additional information to provide realistic and holistic perspectives.

Research Projects: Readers are pointed toward areas of further inquiry connected to each chapter. Suggestions are provided for projects that encourage deeper research and analysis.

Text-Dependent Questions: These questions send the reader back to the text for more careful attention to the evidence presented there.

Series Glossary of Key Terms: This back-of-the book glossary contains terminology used throughout this series. Words found here increase the reader's ability to read and comprehend higher-level books and articles in this field.

Other Titles in This Series

The American Revolution

The Civil War

The Cold War

The Korean War

Native American Wars on the Western Frontier (1866-1890)

US-Led Wars in Iraq, 1991-Present

The Vietnam War

War in Afghanistan: Overthrow of the Taliban and Aftermath

The War of 1812

World War I

World War II

Introduction

By Series Consultant
Lt. Col. Jason R. Musteen

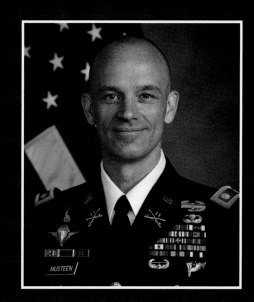

Lt. Col. Jason R. Musteen is a U.S. Army Cavalry officer and combat veteran who has held various command and staff jobs in Infantry and Cavalry units. He holds a PhD in Napoleonic History from Florida State University and currently serves as Chief of the Division of Military History at the U.S. Military Academy at West Point. He has appeared frequently on the History Channel.

Why should middle and high school students read about and study America wars? Does doing so promote militarism or instill misguided patriotism? The United States of America was born at war, and the nation has spent the majority of its existence at war. Our wars have demonstrated both the best and worst of who we are. They have freed millions from oppression and slavery, but they have also been a vehicle for fear, racism, and imperialism. Warfare has shaped the geography of our nation, informed our laws, and it even inspired our national anthem. It has united us and it has divided us.

Valley Forge, the USS *Constitution*, Gettysburg, Wounded Knee, Belleau Wood, Normandy, Midway, Inchon, the A Shau Valley, and Fallujah are all a part of who we are as a nation. Therefore, the study of America at war does not necessarily make students or educators militaristic; rather, it makes them thorough and responsible. To ignore warfare, which has been such a significant part of our history, would not only leave our education incomplete, it would also be negligent.

For those who wish to avoid warfare, or to at least limit its horrors, understanding conflict is a worthwhile, and even necessary, pursuit. The American author John Steinbeck once said, "all war is a symptom of man's failure as a thinking animal." If Steinbeck is right, then we must think. And we must think about war. We must study war with all its attendant horrors and miseries. We must study the heroes and the villains. We must study the root causes of our wars, how we chose to fight them, and what has been achieved or lost through them. The study of America at war is an essential component of being an educated American.

Still, there is something compelling in our military history that makes the study not only necessary, but enjoyable, as well. The desperation that drove Washington's soldiers across the Delaware River at the end of 1776 intensifies an exciting story of American success against all odds. The sailors and Marines who planted the American flag on the rocky peak of Mount Suribachi on Iwo Jima still speak to us of courage and sacrifice. The commitment that led American airmen to the relief of West Berlin in the Cold War inspires us to the service of others. The stories of these men and women are exciting, and they matter. We should study them. Moreover, for all the suffering it brings, war has at times served noble purposes for the United States. Americans can find common pride in the chronicle of the Continental Army's few victories and many defeats in the struggle for independence. We can accept that despite inflicting deep national wounds and lingering division, our Civil War yielded admirable results in the abolition of slavery and eventual national unity. We can celebrate American resolve and character as the nation rallied behind a common cause to free the world from tyranny in World War II. We can do all that without necessarily promoting war.

In this series of books, Mason Crest Publishers offers students a foundation for the study of American wars. Building on the expertise of a team of accomplished authors, the series explores the causes, conduct, and consequences of America's wars. It also presents educators with the means to take their students to a deeper understanding of the material through additional research and project ideas. I commend it to all students and to those who educate them to become responsible, informed Americans.

Chapter 1

The Attack on America

Early on the morning of September 11, 2001, ten Arab men were among the passengers boarding two Boeing 767 passenger jet airplanes at Boston's Logan Airport. Five men boarded each plane, secretly carrying utility knives that were typically used to cut open boxes. Once the jets were in the air, the men used their knives to overpower the pilots and crew. They took control of the jets and steered them south, toward New York City.

Workers search through the debris at Ground Zero, the remains of the World Trade Center in New York City. The September 11 attacks were planned by a terrorist group that was being sheltered in Afghanistan, leading the United States to go to war with

As the airplanes approached New York, the hijackers looked for the city's tallest buildings—the twin towers of the World Trade Center in lower Manhattan. To many people, the towers were a symbol of America's economic strength.

At 8:46 A.M., just as many people were arriving at work, one of the jets passenger jets crashed into the World Trade Center's North Tower. It exploded, and burning jet fuel caused an enormous fire. Some people who were in lower floors were able to evacuate, but hundreds more were trapped inside the building.

Initially, most of the shocked observers thought the plane crash was a tragic accident. They would soon learn that this was not the case. At 9:03 A.M. the second jet crashed into the South Tower. By then it was clear that the morning's events were not accidents but acts of terrorism.

As news spread, Americans were glued to their television sets. But the attack wasn't over. At 9:37 A.M. a third plane, hijacked shortly after taking off from Washington, D.C., crashed into the Pentagon—the headquarters of the U.S. Department of Defense and a symbol of America's military strength—in Arlington, Virginia.

A fourth plane was also hijacked, but when passengers contacted their relatives and emergency personnel by cell phone and were informed of the earlier terrorist incidents, they realized that their plane, too, must be headed toward an important American institution, perhaps even the White House. Heroically, the passengers overwhelmed the hijackers and forced a crash landing in an empty field in Shanksville, Pennsylvania, at

 WORDS TO UNDERSTAND IN THIS CHAPTER

Islamist—a person or group that supports the idea of government based on Muslim laws and doctrines, and is typically hostile toward the influence of Western societies and ideas.

pariah—an outcast; a person or state that is hated by other people.

traumatize—to cause someone to become upset in a way that leads to severe emotional problems.

Smoke billows from the burning World Trade Center shortly after a passenger jet hit the building, September 11, 2001.

10:02 A.M. Everyone on the plane died in the crash. It is believed that the intended target of the fourth plane was either the Capitol, where the U.S. Congress meets, or the White House, where the president resides.

Because all of the hijacked planes had been destined for Los Angeles, they carried thousands of gallons of jet fuel. In New York the explosions and ensuing fires raised the temperature inside the Twin Towers by thousands of degrees. The extreme heat weakened the buildings' structures,

Aerial view of the destruction caused when a hijacked commercial airliner crashed into the Pentagon on September 11, 2001. All 62 people on board the aircraft were killed, along with 125 people in the Pentagon.

and the twin towers soon collapsed, killing everyone still inside—including firemen, policemen, and emergency workers who had rushed into the buildings trying to save trapped workers. The city was showered for blocks around with ash, glass, and soot.

The September 11 attacks were the deadliest foreign attack on U.S. soil in American history. More than 3,000 people were killed that day. Millions of other Americans were ***traumatized*** by the images of the collapsing towers and the charred Pentagon. Financial losses resulting from the attacks were estimated in the hundreds of billions of dollars.

Link to Afghanistan

In the ensuing days, as evidence was collected, American intelligence officials learned that the September 11 attacks had been planned and carried out by members of a group called al-Qaeda, which was led by a man named Osama bin Laden. The al-Qaeda organization had been sheltered in the country of Afghanistan since 1996. The organization operated camps where terrorists were trained, and planned attacks against the United States and other Western countries. The government of Afghanistan supported al-Qaeda's goal of attacking the West.

For many years Afghanistan had been a country in turmoil. Its people had fought against a Soviet invasion during the 1980s, and had waged a civil war during the early 1990s. In 1996 a faction known as the Taliban had gained power in the country. They were *Islamists*, who wanted to establish a state based on Muslim teachings from the seventh century.

In Afghanistan, a Muslim religious student is known as a *talib*. Most supporters of the Taliban had been educated in religious schools, called *madrassas*, that were set up for Afghan boys in Pakistan. The *madrassas* in Pakistan were unlike those in other Muslim countries, however. The teachers were members of a tradition known as Deobandi, which had developed during the nineteenth and early twentieth centuries when Pakistan and India were ruled as a British colony. The Deobandi movement called for a strict interpretation of Islam, and wished to eliminate all foreign influences. Deobandis do not believe in national borders. They claim that a Muslim's only allegiance should be to Allah (god), and that they should be willing to fight for their religion against those who have

President George W. Bush (center) and Secretary of Defense Donald H. Rumsfeld (right) look at satellite images after the September 11 terrorist attack. With them is vice president Richard "Dick" Cheney (left).

different beliefs. Muslims call this *jihad*, or holy war.

Even before the September 11 attacks, the Taliban government had become an international ***pariah*** due to its support for terrorists, violations of human rights, and destruction of cultural treasures.

After the surprise attack, U.S. President George W. Bush declared a "war on terrorism." Afghanistan was the first target. On October 7, 2001, the United States Air Force began bombing sites inside Afghanistan. The American war in Afghanistan had begun.

 # TEXT-DEPENDENT QUESTIONS

1. At what time did the first airplane hit the World Trade Center?
2. Why was the Pentagon targeted by terrorists?
3. What does the Pashto word *talib* mean?

 # RESEARCH PROJECT

Islamism is a political movement in which the government is based on Muslim teachings that date from the seventh century. To Islamists, any developments since the time of the Prophet Muhammad are considered to be corruptions of the proper way to live. Using the Internet or your school library, find some examples of countries that have an Islamist government. Explain how their government is different from the system in the United States today.

Chapter 2

A Country in Turmoil

The origins of the American war in Afghanistan go back decades, and events from centuries ago play an important part. Afghanistan today is a very diverse country. This is because of its location on the major trade routes that passed through central Asia between the historic empires in Persia (Iran) and India. As a result, many different ethnic groups, who speak more than 30 different languages, live in Afghanistan. The largest of these groups are the Pashtun, who make up nearly half of the population. They live primarily in southern and eastern Afghanistan, although Pashtun communities can be found

Soviet troops in armored vehicles patrol a rural area of Afghanistan. The Soviet invasion in 1979 drew international condemnation. Soviet troops remained in the

throughout the country. The Pashtun are a proud people who live by a code of conduct, *Pashtunwali*, that emphasizes honor. The language of the Pashtun, Pashto, is widely spoken in the country.

Other important ethnic groups in Afghanistan are the Tajiks, who mostly live around Herat, a provincial capital in the west, and in northeastern Afghanistan. Uzbeks and Turkmen live in the north, while the Hazara live in Afghanistan's central mountain ranges. Many smaller ethnic groups can be found within the country as well.

Due to Afghanistan's ethnic diversity, it has been difficult for the country to forge a national identity. The Afghan people tend to be more devoted to their tribe and religion than to the nation. Afghans do put aside their ethnic differences to confront outside threats, such as the Soviet invasion and occupation that began in 1979, but this unity tends to disappear once the external threat is removed.

A Country in Turmoil

Due to the recent decades of conflict in Afghanistan, today many Americans view the country as as a backwater where ethnic groups are

 WORDS TO UNDERSTAND IN THIS CHAPTER

boycott—a punitive ban that forbids interaction with certain groups until they change their behavior.

Cold War—a period of tensions between the world's two superpowers, the United States and the Soviet Union, that lasted from 1947 until 1991. The two countries did not fight an open conflict during the Cold War; instead, each tried influence other countries to support its goals and objectives.

colonialism—a policy in which one country directly rules outlying territories and uses their labor and resources to increase its power.

cosmopolitan—a society where aspects of many different cultures are blended easily together.

coup d'état—a sudden, violent, and illegal seizure of power from a government.

exile—to be banned from a native country.

Pakistan is a landlocked country. Modern borders are shown on this map, but in the 1970s Turkmenistan, Uzbekistan, and Tajikistan were part of the Soviet Union.

always fighting and a national government is unable to function properly. However, that was not always the case. From the 1930s to the 1970s, Afghanistan was a poor but stable country. During this time Afghanistan was ruled by a monarch from a Pashtun family. The national government modernized the economy and banking system. It built roads, operated schools, and funded an army and police force. Women were granted the opportunity to work or to earn a college degree. Tourists from neighboring countries, as well as a few adventurers from western nations like the United States or Great Britain, were welcomed in Afghanistan's cities and visited its scenic mountain regions. Kabul, the capital, became known as the "Paris of Central Asia" for its beauty and for the ***cosmopolitan*** lifestyle that could be found there.

During the 1960s and 1970s, Afghanistan received financial assistance from the Soviet Union and the United States, but the country refrained from taking sides in the ***Cold War***. However, the Soviets encouraged the

A street scene in Kabul, 1967. At the time, the city was one of the largest and most prosperous in central Asia.

rise of a Communist political party in Afghanistan, despite the disapproval of King Zahir Shah.

In 1973, when the king was out of the country on a visit to Italy, his cousin Muhammad Daoud and a group of military officers seized control of the government in a ***coup d'état***. Daoud had long been a force in Afghanistan's government, serving as prime minister for many years. He now declared himself president Afghanistan. However, Daoud soon found his newly established government confronted by a rising threat—Islamic fundamentalism, or Islamism.

The movement known as Islamism had developed in response to European ***colonialism***. By the start of the twentieth century, most of the world was controlled by European powers like Great Britain, France, Portugal, the Netherlands, and Germany. In many parts of Africa and Asia, including Afghanistan, most of the people were Muslims, and living under colonial rule caused much resentment and anger. The colonial powers often demanded trading concessions from the territories they ruled, which enabled them to take resources from the lands to maintain the strength of their empires. The colonizers frequently worked with local leaders in the areas they colonized. Many of these leaders were educated in Western universities, where they acquired Western ways of thinking and behaving. Traditional Muslim economic systems were torn apart and rebuilt according to Western norms. Independent artisans and merchants were replaced by factories that provided cheap labor and goods for their colonial masters. Schoolteachers were compelled to teach Western ideas and beliefs and to ignore their native traditions. People who wore traditional clothing rather than Western fashions were ridiculed. Although the colonized people were permitted to practice their traditional religions, colonial governments openly supported Christian missionaries who aggressively sought converts.

As Muslims and Westerners came into closer contact, Islamic societies were constantly pressured to change. Some Islamic religious leaders tried to find ways to adopt Western technology and ideas, while still remaining faithful to their religious heritage. Others advocated for Muslims to break completely with the corrupting influence of the West, and return to a "pure" form of Islam as it was practiced in the seventh century by the Prophet Muhammad and his companions. These people became known as Islamists.

An Islamist group known as the

An Afghan man prays in a mosque in Kabul, circa 1980.

Muslim Brotherhood was originally formed in Egypt during the 1940s, and the organization soon spread to other Muslim countries, including Afghanistan. In the early 1970s, these Muslims protested against the secular government. Daoud had many members of the Muslim Brotherhood arrested and executed.

Although Daoud had originally aligned himself with the Communists, by 1975 he had dismissed the Communists from his government. In 1977 an Afghan national assembly of leaders, called a *loya jirga*, approved Daoud's new constitution, which created a presidential, one-party political system for the country.

In April of 1978 Afghan Communists joined with officers in Afghanistan's army and air force to stage another coup. President Daoud and his family was killed in what became known as the Saur Revolution. The communist People's Democratic Party of Afghanistan (PDPA) seized power, led by Nur Muhammad Taraki. The PDPA government immediately announced major reforms to Afghan society that were in line with communist and socialist principles, such as greater rights for women. This angered many conservative and religious Afghans, many of whom were also upset because communism discourages the practice of Islam and other religions. The PDPA also attempted to divide tribal land among small farmers and tried to set up farming cooperatives, such as the Soviet Union and other communist countries had. This policy was extremely unpopular in Afghanistan. The PDPA also targeted members of Afghanistan's middle and upper classes. Thousands of them were killed, and many more were driven into *exile*.

Afghan exiles soon began organizing in neighboring Pakistan and Iran to resist the Communists. However, the PDPA government was dealing with its own internal problems. A few months after the Saur Revolution, Taraki was murdered by supporters of a rival leader, Hafizullah Amin.

Although Amin was also a communist, he tried to win the support of Afghan Muslim leaders by discontinuing some of the state's anti-religious policies. However, these measures did little to erase hostility among the population.

Meanwhile, Soviet leaders in Moscow were very concerned about events in Afghanistan. The Soviets feared that if Amin's government did

Soviet soldiers ride an armored vehicle through the streets of Kabul. During the Soviet occupation, about 5 million Afghans became refugees in Pakistan.

not placate the Muslim population, Islamists would be able to overthrow the government and establish an Islamic theocracy. This had occurred in neighboring Iran during late 1978 and early 1979. Ayatollah Khomeini, leader of the Iranian Revolution, was strongly critical of the Soviet Union, which bordered both Iran and Afghanistan. The Soviet states (called Soviet socialist republics, or SSR) in central Asia all had large Muslim populations. Soviet officials feared that people in states like the Kazakh SSR, Kirgiz SSR, Tajik SSR, Turkmen SSR, and Uzbek SSR might revolt against Soviet leadership if Islamists gained control in Afghanistan.

During the last days of December 1979, the Soviet Union invaded Afghanistan. Soviet troops captured Kabul, executed Amin, and installed Babrak Karmal, a moderate Afghan communist, in his place. Karmal had been a member of the PDPA who had been forced into exile by Amin.

War With the Soviets

Resistance to the Soviet occupation grew quickly. Leaders appealed to all Afghans on the basis of their Muslim and tribal identity. The fighters who resisted became known as *mujahideen*, which means "those waging

An Afghan mujahideen demonstrates how to use a hand-held surface-to-air missile.

jihad." The *mujahideen* considered the Soviet invaders to be "godless" and repressive of their religion.

The United Nations, as well as many individual countries, condemned the invasion of Afghanistan. The United States in particular strongly protested against the move by its Cold War rival. The U.S. had lost an important regional ally when Iran's government was toppled by Khomeini's revolution in early 1979, and President Jimmy Carter considered the Soviet invasion an attempt to reshape the fragile balance of power in Asia and the Middle East. President Carter declared an economic embargo against the Soviet Union, cancelling sales of American wheat to Moscow. He also declared that American athletes would boycott the 1980 Olympic Games in Moscow.

The U.S. government also wanted to help the Afghans that were resisting the Soviet invasion. The Carter administration secretly sent money and weapons to Pakistan, which in turn passed them on to the *mujahideen*.

After Ronald Reagan took office as president of the United States in

1981, the covert U.S. support for the Afghan rebels increased. A U.S. congressman from Texas named Charlie Wilson was the rebels' biggest champion in Congress. He was able to increase funding for the *mujahideen* each year, from about $20 million in 1980 to more than $630 million in 1987. Wilson and operatives from the CIA also arranged for Saudi Arabia to match the U.S. aid to the *mujahideen*. Pakistan's president, Zia ul-Haq, allowed the Afghan rebels to train at secret bases near the Pakistani city of Peshawar and elsewhere. Pakistan's Directorate for Inter-Services Intelligence (ISI), the country's main spy agency, distributed the funds and weapons to various *mujahideen* groups and were responsible for the training programs.

Thanks to this covert aid, *mujahideen* groups within Afghanistan had increasing success ambushing Soviet troops in the rugged countryside. U.S.-supplied, shoulder-fired Stinger missiles took a heavy toll on Soviet aircraft. The Soviets responded brutally, targeting especially the rural Afghan population, even noncombatants. In many instances entire villages were annihilated.

Afghan mujahideen return to their village, which has been destroyed by Soviet forces in reprisal for a mujahideen attack

As the casualties on both sides mounted, Karmal resigned and was succeeded by another Communist, Muhammad Najibullah. Although Najibullah promised to respect Islam, the *mujahideen* rebuffed his offers of a settlement.

By the mid-1980s the Afghan occupation had become extremely costly for the Soviet Union, and was highly unpopular as well. When a new Soviet leader, Mikhail Gorbachev, came to power in 1985 with plans to restructure and reform the U.S.S.R's economy and political system, he recognized that for his proposals to succeed the Soviet Union would need to withdraw from Afghanistan.

In April 1988 the governments of Pakistan and Afghanistan—with the Soviet Union and the United States acting as guarantors—reached an agreement to settle the Afghan conflict. Under the terms of the agreement, the Soviet Union would withdraw its troops, refugees would be permitted to return home without fear of persecution, and Afghanistan would become a neutral state. The *mujahideen* accepted the agreement, and by February 1989 all Soviet troops had left the country.

 TEXT-DEPENDENT QUESTIONS

1. What was the nickname for Kabul in the 1960s and early 1970s? Why?
2. What Islamist group did Muhammad Daoud persecute during his reign?
3. What does the word *mujahideen* mean?

 **RESEARCH PROJECT**

Using the Internet or your school library, find out about Charlie Wilson, a U.S. congressman from Texas who used his position to increase the covert support provided to the muhajideen during the Soviet invasion. Write a report and present it to your class.

Chapter 3

Civil War in Afghanistan

A fghanistan was devastated by the Soviet occupation. It is estimated that a million Afghans lost their lives during conflict, while about 5 million people fled the country as refugees. Afghanistan's economy was shattered, its infrastructure in ruins. Unexploded land mines littered much of the countryside.

After the Soviet withdrawal, the *mujahideen* continued to attack Najibullah's Afghan forces. Najibullah declared a national emergency and the Soviet Union

An ethnic Uzbek soldier loyal to northern Afghani warlord General Rashid Dostum sits atop a mobile rocket launcher just north of Kabul in October 1996. During the 1990s, a variety of Afghan factions battle for control of the country.

At the end of the Soviet occupation, Afghanistan was covered with metal scraps and live munitions, such as this land mine.

sent in huge shipments of military and economic aid. With this help, the army was able to beat back *mujahideen* attacks on the cities for a while. By 1991, however, the Najibullah government controlled only about 10 percent of Afghanistan. The next year, Najibullah fled the country as an alliance of *mujahideen* captured Kabul.

In April 1992, nearly all of the *mujahideen* groups signed the Peshawar Accord, a peace plan that called for a transitional government. In this government, for two years power would be shared among the various groups until national elections could be held. However, one *mujahideen* group held out. Known as Hezb-e Islami, it was led by a warlord named Gulbuddin Hekmatyar. During the struggle against the Soviet Union, Hekmatyar, a Pashtun tribesman and an Islamist, had been a favored recipient of aid from Pakistan. His organization had received more of the U.S. and Saudi funds and weapons than any other *mujahideen* group. Now, he saw an opportunity to rule the entire country, and Pakistan's government saw an opportunity to install a **client** who would support their interests as the head of Afghanistan's government.

In April 1992 Hezb-e Islami attempted to seize control of Kabul, but the other *mujahideen* groups joined forces and drove him away from the city. They were led by Ahmad Shah Massoud, a military leader who during the Soviet occupation had gained fame as the "Lion of the Panjshir Valley" for his role in driving the Soviets out of northern Afghanistan. In

 WORDS TO UNDERSTAND IN THIS CHAPTER

client—a person who is dependent on a more powerful person or country for political or economic power.

extortion—the practice of obtaining money through force or threats.

Members of a mujahideen faction prepare to fight for Kabul, 1990s.

May, Hekmatyar's artillery began shelling the capital city. This would touch off four years of civil war, as the *mujahideen* fought with Hekmatyar as well as with each other. Afghanistan was split into small territories held by rival *mujahideen* factions, usually dominated by a local warlord. Rival warlords profited from drug trafficking and were accused of **extortion**, kidnapping, burglary, and rampant violence against women. Kabul and other cities were the site of most fighting; the capital was turned into rubble by repeated bombardments.

Northern Alliance leader Ahmed Shah Massood, center, gives directions to his troops during a battle for a mountain pass south of Mazar-e Sharif in October 1996. A veteran of the war against the Soviets, Massood was one of the most respected of the mujahideen leaders.

By 1994, the government of Pakistan had given up on its idea that Hekmatyar could control the country. The Hezb-e Islami organization did not have enough popular support to be effective. Instead, Pakistan began to support another group of militants, known as the Taliban.

Rise of the Taliban

The Taliban was started by a man named Muhammad Omar, a Pashtun from a rural area in Afghanistan's Kandahar Province. Little is known about Omar's life, but he fought against the Soviets during the 1980s. He lost an eye during one battle. When the Soviet occupation ended, Omar moved to Pakistan, where he taught in a *madrassa* and was exposed to the Deobandi tradition. He later returned to Kandahar Province, opening a *madrassa* in Singesar.

In early 1994, Omar and about 50 of his students (in the Pashto language, *talib*) armed themselves and began to fight back against the corruption and excesses of warlords in his region. The Afghan people were tired of crime, and they supported Omar's efforts to end crime and enforce Islamic laws. The Taliban's success drew other students to join Omar's group. Pakistan's ISI also provided military training and financial support to the organization. By November 1994, the Taliban was in control of the entire Kandahar Province. It declared the region under its control to be the Islamic Emirate of Afghanistan.

The Taliban continued to spread its area of control throughout the country. Taliban forces captured Herat in September 1995, and gained control over Jalalabad and Kabul in 1996. They deposed the interim president, Burhanuddin Rabbani, and removed the transitional government from power. Gulbuddin Hekmatyar fled Afghanistan to live in exile in Iran. Three countries—Pakistan, Saudi Arabia, and the United Arab Emirates—soon recognized the Taliban as the legitimate government of Afghanistan.

Government of the Taliban

Under Omar's leadership, the Taliban was initially quite popular with the Afghan people, who were weary from years of chaos and abuses at the hands of the warlords. The Taliban was able to restore order in the areas

The Taliban required women to cover themselves completely in a burqa *when out in public. Those who did not comply with the strict laws were beaten or killed.*

of the country that it controlled, and reopened roads that had been closed due to fighting. However, the Taliban also implemented a strict version of *Sharia*, or Islamic law. They prohibited computers, movies, televisions, and radios, claiming these exerted an anti-Islamic influence. They also banned music, photography, paintings, sculpture, and any picture of humans or animals. They established laws requiring men to wear beards at least a fist-length below the chin. Improper beard lengths might result in a public beating. Those convicted of theft might have a hand or foot amputated, while those arrested for murder and certain other crimes were publicly executed.

But the Taliban's most stringent laws affected women and girls. Afghan girls were not permitted to attend school, and women could no longer hold jobs, which caused an employment crisis in education and health care. In public, women were required to wear the *burqa*, a garment that covers the entire body, with only a crocheted section over the eyes through which to see. Designed to enforce the Muslim custom of secluding women from men, the *burqa* had long been worn by some religious women in Afghanistan, but the Taliban made it a requirement for all women. Those caught not wearing one were subject to extreme punishment. Women caught outside their home without being accompanied by a male relative could be beaten or shot. A woman caught wearing fingernail polish could have her fingertips chopped off. Executions and punishments such as flogging took place publicly in Afghan soccer stadiums.

The Taliban also destroyed important pieces of Afghanistan's cultural heritage. These included artifacts from the National Museum in Kabul, historical sites in Ghazni, and a pair of enormous ancient statues of

Two enormous pre-Islamic Buddha statues in Bamiyan were carved from the rock during the sixth century; they were destroyed by the Taliban in March 2001.

Osama bin Laden had fought with the mujahideen *in Afghanistan during the Soviet occupation. He wished to rid Muslim countries of Western influences.*

Buddha in Bamiyan Province. The regime ignored the international outcry that resulted from such actions.

The Taliban's status as an international pariah was solidified by its policy of permitting terrorist organizations to operate training camps in Afghanistan. Among these groups was al-Qaeda, which shared the Taliban's worldview about the destructive influence of Western culture on Muslim communities. Like the Taliban, al-Qaeda's leaders wanted to replace secular governments with Islamist regimes.

Al-Qaeda's founder, a wealthy Saudi named Osama bin Laden, had first gone to Afghanistan during the 1980s, to join the *mujahideen* in their fight against the Soviet occupation. In that effort he indirectly received aid from both Saudi Arabia and the United States. But by the early 1990s bin Laden had become a fierce opponent of the Saudi monarchy and the United States. Five years after fleeing Saudi Arabia in 1991, he settled in Afghanistan, where the Taliban provided him sanctuary and he supported the Taliban financially.

Al-Qaeda was involved in several attacks against American targets, including the August 1998 bombing of the U.S. embassies in Kenya and Tanzania. The attacks killed 224 people and injured more than 4,000. In response, about two weeks later the U.S. military launched 75 cruise missiles at four camps in Afghanistan where terrorists were being trained.

During 1999 and 2000, the United Nations Security Council passed resolutions demanding that the Taliban close all terrorist training camps in Afghanistan and hand over bin Laden for trial, but the Taliban refused.

Conflict Continues in Afghanistan

Although the Taliban controlled most of Afghanistan, a coalition of diverse opposition groups called the Northern Alliance held substantial pieces of territory in the north. Unlike the Taliban, which was composed largely of members of the Pashtun tribe, the Northern Alliance represent-

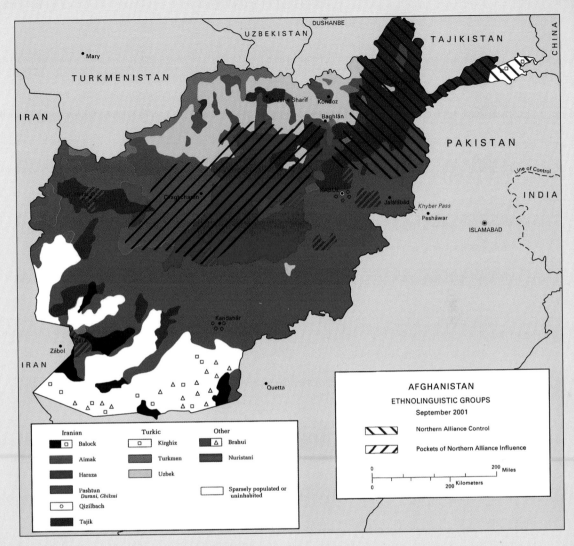

This U.S. Army map shows the extent of territory controlled by the Northern Alliance at the time of Ahmad Shah Massood's death in September 2001.

ed Afghanistan's minority tribes—the Tajiks, Hazara, Uzbeks, and Turkmen. It was led by the former president Burhanuddin Rabbani and the former defense minister Ahmad Shah Massoud, both ethnic Tajiks. Another leader was Abdul Rashid Dostum, a warlord who controlled an army of about 50,000 Uzbeks.

Between 1996 and 2000, the Taliban was able to drive off most of these groups, thanks to generous financial support from Pakistan and Saudi Arabia, as well as from bin Laden. More than 80,000 Pakistani students also went to Afghanistan to fight with the Taliban. Ahmad Shah Massoud's militia was the only one able to defend its northern region from Taliban invasions. The organization tried to get Massoud to stop fighting and join their government, but he refused. He disagreed with the Taliban's fundamentalist approach, and wanted to build a democratic Afghanistan in which all people were represented.

On September 9, 2001, two Arabs posing as journalists assassinated Ahmed Shah Massood. They had hidden a bomb inside of their camera, and detonated it while purporting to interview the Tajik leader. Two days after the murder of Massood, al-Qaeda terrorists hijacked four American jetliners and carried out the suicide attacks on the World Trade Center in New York City and the Pentagon outside Washington, D.C.

 TEXT-DEPENDENT QUESTIONS

1. What *mujahideen* leader refused to take part in the government created by the Peshawar Accord?
2. Who was known as the "Lion of the Panjshir Valley?"
3. What event caused the United States to launch cruise missile attacks against targets in Afghanistan during August 1998?

 RESEARCH PROJECT

The AK-47 was one of the most common automatic rifles used by the Soviet Union and its allies. By the end of the Soviet occupation, Afghans possessed hundreds of thousands of these weapons. Do some research on this type of firearm. What was the range, and how accurate were these weapons? Were there any limitations or drawbacks to using them? Why were they so popular? Write a one-page report on what you learn.

آیا دا فکر کوی چه تاسی محفوظ یاست

هل الفاعده ـ هل تظنوا انکم امنین.

Chapter 4

Bringing Down the Taliban

Blame for the September 11 attacks quickly fell on Osama bin Laden's al-Qaeda organization. On September 20, U.S. president George W. Bush demanded that the Taliban turn over bin Laden and other al-Qaeda leaders. The Taliban refused, insisting that the United States would have to provide detailed proof of al-Qaeda's involvement. The Bush administration considered this a delaying tactic. On October 7, U.S. and British forces began an aerial campaign of bombing al-Qaeda camps and Taliban military ***strongholds***.

Detail from an American psychological operations (Psy-ops) leaflet dropped over Taliban defenders in the Tora Bora region. The Afghan men pictured in the cave have noticed an American missile headed their way; the caption (in both Pashto and Arabic) says, "Taliban, do you think that you are safe..."

Muhammad Omar and the Taliban may have believed that the United States would not be willing to send ground troops to Afghanistan. The U.S. cruise missile strikes in 1998 had failed to cause any long-lasting damage to al-Qaeda, and without soldiers on the ground the U.S. would not be able to hunt terrorists or overthrow the Taliban regime. If the U.S. did send soldiers, they would face many challenges. Afghanistan is an immense, land-locked country, with massive mountain ranges and remote valleys in the north and east, and near desert-like conditions on the plains to the south and west. Winter was approaching, and mountain passes would be virtually impassible. Even air support was often adversely affected by the winds and storms of the harsh Afghan climate. The rough terrain had been one of the major obstacles the Soviet troops faced during their war, and it would make the U.S. military task difficult.

Nonetheless, the United States began preparing to operate inside Afghanistan. They first arranged with the government of Uzbekistan, a former Soviet republic that gained independence when the U.S.S.R. broke apart in 1992, to use a former Soviet airbase near Karshi Kandabad. In late September 2001 U.S. *special forces* were sent to Uzbekistan, along with the the 1st battalion of the 87th Infantry, 10th Mountain Division. British forces were also sent to Afghanistan in support of the American troops.

The U.S. plan was for American special forces to provide support to the Northern Alliance, and work with them to overthrow the Taliban regime. The U.S. contacted three of the main Northern Alliance leaders, and encouraged them to expand the areas under their control, with U.S. help, and to provide bases for subsequent operations. These leaders included the Uzbek leader Abdul Rashid Dostum, as well as Mohammed

 WORDS TO UNDERSTAND IN THIS CHAPTER

special forces—elite units within the U.S. military that are highly trained in guerrilla warfare.
stronghold—a place that has been fortified and made difficult to attack.

Mohammad Fahim Khan (left) escorts U.S. Secretary of Defense Donald H. Rumsfeld past an honor guard in Kabul. Fahim was an ethnic Tajik, and a protege of Ahmad Shah Massood.

Fahim and Mohammed Daud. For political purposes, the special forces teams were divided among the various factions of the Northern Alliance as equally as possible, because the United States did not want to give the impression of favoring one of these longtime rivals who were now allied against the Taliban.

War Begins in Northern Afghanistan

The first special forces teams arrived in Afghanistan on October 14. They were brought by helicopter, at night, to Mazar-e Sharif, where Dostum's Uzbek forces had gathered. Half of the special forces team worked with Dostum to plan an attack on Mazar-e Sharif, riding on horseback into the mountains around the city. The other half of the team was assigned to direct airstrikes by American B-1 and B-52 bombers, as well as by F-14, F-15, F-16, and F-18 fighter-bombers. The American aircraft attacked Taliban positions in the nearby Alma Tak Mountains, destroying Taliban troops and their camps, as well as armored vehicles and artillery.

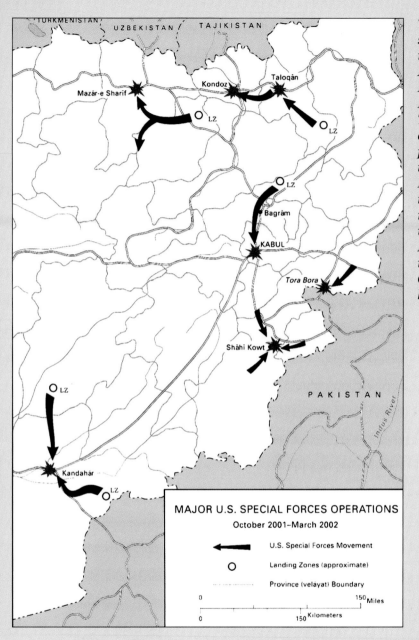

MAJOR U.S. SPECIAL FORCES OPERATIONS
October 2001–March 2002

←	U.S. Special Forces Movement
○	Landing Zones (approximate)
....	Province (velāyat) Boundary

The Americans landed special forces teams into three areas: Mazar-e Sharif, Bagram airfield and Kabul, and Kondoz-Taloqan. Once these areas were secured, the plan was to move teams to liberate Kandahar, the center of the Taliban government. Then the focus would shift to the Tora Bora Mountains, where it was believed that al-Qaeda leaders were hiding.

The airstrikes had an immediate psychological effect on the Taliban, causing panic and fear, while at the same time encouraging Dostum's militia. At first the Taliban responded by reinforcing its troops, but that merely provided new targets for the American aircraft.

With the Taliban's ability to wage war compromised, the survivors fled north to Mazar-e Sharif. In pursuit, Dostum's forces began to conduct old-fashioned cavalry charges into the northern Darya Suf and Balkh Valleys.

American special forces partici-
pated in these assaults, even riding into battle on horseback. At
the same time, B-52 bombers
continued to pound the retreating
Taliban forces.

On November 10, Dostum's
forces gained control of Mazar-e
Sharif. As his troops marched
into the city, they were greeted by
cheering Afghans. The capture of
Mazar-e Sharif was the first
major victory for the U.S.-led
coalition in the war in
Afghanistan.

The Capture of Kabul

On October 19, a second team of
U.S. special forces had been sent
to northeastern Afghanistan,
where Northern Alliance con-

*Teams of U.S. Army special forces assisted the
Northern Alliance forces by directing airstrikes
against Taliban positions. Each day American aircraft circled the areas where the Northern Alliance
was operating. This enabled the fight to be waged
with only a small number of U.S. soldiers.*

trolled a former Soviet air base at Bagram and protected the passage to
the Panjshir Valley, a stronghold of Ahmed Shah Massood's forces. The
Tajik militia was now commanded by Mohammed Fahim. Once the
Americans arrived, they began directing airstrikes against Taliban positions on the nearby Shamali Plains to the south of the Panjshir Valley. For
the next three weeks, American aircraft pounded Taliban and al-Qaeda
military positions, killing hundreds of their front-line troops.

The Taliban forces were so weakened by the U.S. airstrikes that
Northern Alliance decided to quickly assault Kabul. On November 13,
they launched an attack on the city. The defenders quickly gave up the
city. Some fled south to the Taliban stronghold in Kandahar; others went
east to the Tora Bora Mountains. On November 14, General Fahim's army
occupied Kabul, and by early December the U.S. Embassy was reopened
in the capital city.

Northern Alliance troops under General Dostum's command in Mazar-e Sharif take a break on a wall near they city's busiest street. The Northern Alliance captured the city on November 10, 2001.

Battles for Taloqan and Kondoz

As Taliban forces abandoned their positions in the northeast and north-west sections of the country, the focus of the war shifted to the area around Taloqan and Kondoz. Special forces teams had arrived in the area on November 8 to help the militia commanded by Mohammed Daud. However, Daud did not wait for American airstrikes, and his forces captured the city of Taloqan with little trouble on November 11.

As Daud's militia advanced west toward the city of Kondoz, the American special forces once again assisted by guiding airstrikes against Taliban defensive positions. Between November 13 and November 23, the airstrikes destroyed 12 Taliban tanks, 51 trucks, and many defensive bunkers, while killing about 2,000 Taliban soldiers. On November 23, the Taliban defenders surrendered Kondoz.

During the Mazar-e Sharif and Taloqan-Kondoz campaigns, the Northern Alliance and American forces freed six Afghan provinces from

Taliban control. They did all of this in about a month with only a few U.S. casualties, while inflicting thousands of casualties on the enemy and destroying Taliban and al-Qaeda defensive positions.

Even while the fighting was underway, a humanitarian effort had begun to help the people living in the northern region. C-17 cargo aircraft dropped hundreds of thousands of food packets from the skies to refugee camps. The work of rebuilding the war-torn country began even while the campaign to retake the remainder of Afghanistan continued.

U.S. Army special forces ride horseback alongside Afghan members of the Northern Alliance during a patrol in the fall of 2001.

The American Presence Increases

Before the war in Afghanistan began, American leaders had decided to limit the number of U.S. troops in Afghanistan. They wanted to avoid the appearance of a U.S. occupation that would stir up resistance as the Soviet occupation had. However, with the early successes of the Northern Alliance, the Pentagon decided to increase the small U.S. troop commitment in Afghanistan by a few hundred soldiers.

During the Northern Alliance campaign in the north, U.S. forces also struck in the southern part of the country, in the heart of Taliban country near Kandahar. On October 20, about 200 U.S. Rangers parachuted into a landing zone to the southwest of Kandahar and quickly captured a Taliban base and airstrip. In late November, this would become the site of Camp Rhino, the first U.S. Marine Corps base in Afghanistan. The United States and its Afghan allies also began to repair the infrastructure of northern Afghanistan, so that military supplies and humanitarian aid could reach the region from Uzbekistan and other countries. This work was completed by late December, enabling future military operations to proceed.

In December 2001, before the fighting ended, Hamid Karzai was chosen to lead the interim government of Afghanistan.

There were activities going on outside the country as well. In early December, the United Nations sponsored a meeting to discuss the future of Afghanistan in Bonn, Germany. Representatives from the major Afghan opposition and exile groups took part. The group decided to establish an interim administration that would govern the country until democratic elections could be held. They selected Hamid Karzai, an ethnic Pashtun who had fought with the *mujahideen* against the Soviets, to preside over the interim government. Karzai's father had been a member of the Afghan Parliament during the 1970s, and was the head of a powerful Pashtun clan with long ties to the monarchy. Karzai was also a supporter of the West and an opponent of the Taliban.

The Attack on Kandahar

The city of Kandahar was the next U.S. objective. Military planners suspected that it would be the hardest city to capture. It was a long way from the areas where the Northern Alliance had the most support. The people of Kandahar were primarily Pashtuns, and this region had been the starting point for the Taliban movement.

As they had in the north, American special forces teams entered the region and linked up with anti-Taliban resistance groups near Kandahar. One of these was a small militia led by Hamid Karzai. On November 16, the special forces were able to call in airstrikes that halted a Taliban attack on Karzai's men near the village of Tarin Kowt. With U.S. equipment and training, Karzai's militia grew from about 35 men to nearly 800. In early December, his army moved south toward the village of Sayd Alim Kalay, where an important bridge on the route to Kandahar was located. Around this time, Karzai learned that he had been chosen as head of the interim government of Afghanistan.

Karzai's forces quickly routed the small force of Taliban soldiers holding the village near the eastern end of the bridge, but they could not take the well-defended bridge itself. For the next two days, despite constant attacks by American fighter-bombers, the Taliban successfully defended the crossing. Taliban counterattacks were turned back by Karzai's soldiers, supported by U.S. airstrikes. After another attack on December 4, the Taliban forces finally withdrew. On December 6, Karzai negotiated the surrender of Kandahar by Taliban forces.

At the same time, another Pashtun militia led by Gul Sharzai, the former governor of Kandahar, was advancing on the city from the south. After heaving fighting to reach the city, Sharzai's men captured the Kandahar Airport on December 7 without a fight. The Taliban had evacuated the city. Sharzai moved into the city, and Karzai named him gover-

The capture of Kandahar Airport provided a base for U.S. aircraft, such as this F-16.

nor of Kandahar. The capture of Kandahar Airport would give the U.S. another way to ship supplies into Afghanistan. The anti-Taliban forces now controlled every major city in Afghanistan.

The Assault on Tora Bora

After the fall of Kabul, al-Qaeda and Taliban forces had retreated to the Tora Bora Mountains south of Jalalabad, near the Pakistani border. This region contains some of the most rugged terrain in the world, and the terrorists had built fortifications and dug caves throughout Tora Bora. With large numbers of well-supplied, fanatical al-Qaeda fighters dug into extensive fortified positions, Tora Bora was expected to be an extremely tough target.

As with other areas, the U.S. would rely on Afghan fighters supported by American special forces. Local warlord Hazrat Ali had an ethnically mixed army, which would assault the Taliban and al-Qaeda defenses in Tora Bora. Special forces teams would help by providing advice and aerial support. The soldiers could not reach the enemy stronghold in trucks; they had to move on foot, with burros carrying their equipment and ammunition along narrow mountain paths.

The attack on Tora Bora began with an aerial bombardment on December 5 that lasted several days. Once Hazrat Ali's men were in place,

Reverse side of the psy-ops leaflet pictured on page 33 that was dropped on Tora Bora; the caption completes the statement from the front, "Taliban, do you think that you are safe..." by adding, "in your tomb?"

Tora Bora is a cave complex situated in the White Mountains (Safed Koh) of eastern Afghanistan. The rough terrain made Tora Bora difficult to attack.

they began to assault the cave defenders. Each day, Ali's forces would advance into the canyon, and each evening they would fall back. Much of the same ground would have to be captured again the next day. This went on for eight days and nights. Finally, on December 17, the last of the defenders were overrun. The U.S. special forces soldiers searched the caves into January, but by that point the Taliban and al-Qaeda leaders had escaped across the border into Pakistan.

For that reason, the Battle of Tora Bora is generally considered a failure of the American strategy in Afghanistan. Critics of the U.S. commander, General Tommy Franks, say that rather than trusting the Afghan forces, U.S. troops should have been used to attack the caves. These critics believe American troops could have done a better job of guarding the border with Pakistan to preventing Osama bin Laden and other leaders from escaping. American commanders in Afghanistan, including the top CIA agent in the country, had requested a large 800-man force to do this job. But General Franks wanted to maintain the strategy of relying on the Afghans, as that had worked well in the conquest of the cities.

General Tommy R. Franks (left) the U.S. commander in Afghanistan, speaks to reporters at the Pentagon with Secretary of Defense Donald H. Rumsfeld. After the Battle of Tora Bora, Franks and Rumsfeld were criticized for not sending U.S. troops to ensure that Osama bin Laden and other al-Qaeda and Taliban leaders could not escape from the region.

Nonetheless, with the capture of Kabul and Kandahar and the destruction of organized resistance in Tora Bora, Afghanistan was now in effect liberated. It had taken fewer than sixty days of concentrated military operations and only a few hundred American soldiers to seize the country from the Taliban and its terrorist allies.

 TEXT-DEPENDENT QUESTIONS

1. What were some of the challenges the U.S. military faced in fighting a conflict in Afghanistan?
2. What was the first major city captured by the Northern Alliance with the assistance of U.S. special forces?
3. What Afghan warlord's forces were involved in the attack on Tora Bora?

 **RESEARCH PROJECT**

Go online and find the indictment of Zacarias Moussaoui, who was alleged to be a member of the September 11 terrorist attack team. Read the section on the indictment that provides background information on al-Qaeda. What are four reasons that the terrorist organization began to encourage attacks against the United States during the 1990s?

Chapter 5

Resurgence
of the Taliban

Although bin Laden had escaped, the defeat of the Taliban handicapped al-Qaeda's ability to launch new terrorist attacks. The group had lost its training facilities in Afghanistan, and its leaders were forced to hide out. The U.S. government soon launched a global effort to cut off al-Qaeda's funding sources and arrest or kill its leaders.

In Afghanistan, there was still much work to be done. The U.S. military worked to provide humanitarian aid to Afghans. It also focused on finding and

Afghanis haul off humanitarian aid provided by the International Red Cross. The United States and many other countries provided aid to the war-torn country.

destroying the remnants of Taliban and al-Qaeda forces in Afghanistan. This was easier said than done, as it was easy for enemy militants to hide in the vast and mountainous country. Another objective of the U.S. military was to build a true Afghan army that would support the national government. A disciplined and well-trained army could prevent enemy forces from escaping battle sites, as they had at Tora Bora.

 WORDS TO UNDERSTAND IN THIS CHAPTER

counterinsurgency—military or political action taken against the activities of guerrillas or rebels.

mandate—the authority to carry out a policy or course of action.

mortar—a short, smoothbore gun that fires bombs at high angles.

In early 2002, the focus of the military effort shifted to the south and west of Tora Bora, to the Paktia Province and the cities of Gardez and Zormat. The people in this area were mostly Pashtuns, and many sympathized with the Taliban. When military planners learned that around 200 Taliban and al-Qaeda fighters had concentrated in the Shahi Kowt Valley, they launched Operation Anaconda in March 2002.

The Shahi Kowt Valley is approximately 8,000 feet in elevation, with the surrounding peaks exceeding 11,000 feet. The valley's higher eastern mountain range is pierced by only a few main routes and dozens of smaller goat paths. Near the southern end is a mountain peak called Takur Ghar with excellent observation over both the valley and a number of the exit routes. All in all, the valley was surrounded by formidable terrain, making the area to isolate. The plan was to isolate and surround enemy escape routes, then strike hard against the enemy defenses.

For this operation, the U.S. military sent more than 1,500 soldiers to the Shahi Kowt Valley, where they worked with about 1,000 Afghan soldiers. The Taliban and al-Qaeda fighters had prepared strong defensive positions, and they fired fired **mortars** and heavy machine guns at the attacking forces. At the battle of Battle of Takur Ghar on March 3-4, several American helicopters were shot down and a number of Americans killed. The Americans soon realized that they had underestimated the size of the Taliban force. There were actually more than 500 enemy fighters hiding in the mountainous valley.

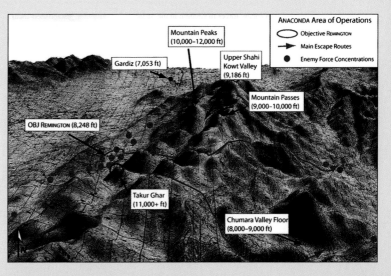

ANACONDA Area of Operations
- Objective REMINGTON
- Main Escape Routes
- Enemy Force Concentrations

Mountain Peaks (10,000–12,000 ft)

Gardiz (7,053 ft)

Upper Shahi Kowt Valley (9,186 ft)

Mountain Passes (9,000–10,000 ft)

OBJ REMINGTON (8,248 ft)

Takur Ghar (11,000+ ft)

Chumara Valley Floor (8,000–9,000 ft)

This U.S. military map shows the elevation of the Shahi Kowt Valley, which is approximately 3 miles (5 km) wide and 6 miles (10 km) long.

(Above) A U.S. soldier takes a photo of Soviet-era ammunition that was discovered in Afghanistan. As U.S. troops gained control of the country, they oversaw the destruction of many old rockets and weapons that the Soviets had left behind.
(Opposite) American soldiers patrol a rocky region looking for Taliban and al-Qaeda fighters. Small bands of fighters maintained a stubborn resistance.

By March 16, the fighting was over. The Pentagon estimated that hundreds of enemy fighters had been killed, although independent reports would call that figure into question. Many of the al-Qaeda and Taliban fighters were able to flee into the surrounding hills, then cross the border to safe havens in the tribal regions of Pakistan.

At this point, the major fighting in the initial conflict was done. However, for the next 12 years U.S. and British military troops would remain in Afghanistan to support attempts to ensure political stability and to help rebuild the nation.

A New Government

The December 2001 Bonn Conference established a temporary government known as the Afghan Interim Authority (AIA). It was headed by Hamid Karzai, and featured a 30-member cabinet that represented all of Afghanistan's ethnic groups and included two women. The agreement specified that a transitional government should be in place within six months.called for a commission to write a new constitution and another to establish a new Afghan justice system based on international legal standards, the rule of law, Islamic principles, and Afghan legal traditions.

An Afghan elder shows his purple inked finger to indicate that he voted during the Presidential and Provincial Council elections in Barg e Matal, Nuristan Province.

In June 2002, a 1,050-member *loya jirga* convened to create a new parliament. The *loya jirga* elected Hamid Karzai president of the Transitional Islamic State of Afghanistan (TISA). According to terms agreed to at the Bonn Conference, the TISA was then to hold another *loya jirga* within 18 months to adopt a constitution and, within 24 months, to hold nationwide elections for a permanent government.

In 2003, the constitution was approved by a constitutional *loya jirga*, which included 502 members, most of them elected representatives. The new constitution created a democratic form of government similar in many respects to that of the United States.

In a national election on October 9, 2004, Karzai was elected president with 55 percent of the vote. There were more than a dozen candidates in the race, including Abdul Dostum and the ethnic Tajik Yunus Qanuni, an associate of Ahmad Shah Massoud. Taliban rebels tried to disrupt the election with a campaign of bombings and assassinations. Nonetheless, it is believed that about 75 percent of eligible Afghans voted in the 2004 presidential election. The next year, Afghanistan's first democratic assembly was elected. To many observers, Afghanistan finally seemed to be on a path to stability and prosperity.

Yet optimism waned as Karzai's administration failed to adequately combat Afghanistan's problems. Even after his electoral victory, President Karzai's national government exercised only limited control outside the capital city. The Taliban reemerged as a dangerous force, particularly in the south-central region around Kandahar. Taliban attacks slowed reconstruction efforts and convinced some international aid agencies to pull their workers out of Afghanistan. And al-Qaeda fighters continued to find safe haven along the Afghanistan-Pakistan border.

NATO Takes a Leading Role

The 2001 Bonn Conference also created the International Security Assistance Force (ISAF) in Afghanistan. The purpose of this international military force was to help the new Afghan government support the reconstruction of Afghanistan. At first the United States and Great Britain took the lead in the ISAF, but in August 2003 the North Atlantic Treaty Organization (NATO) took over the leadership role. NATO is a political-military alliance of the United States and several dozen European states.

French soldiers, serving with NATO forces in Afghanistan as part of the International Security Assistance Force, return to their base after completing a security patrol in Kapisa Province, 2008.

Beginning in 2005, unmanned aerial vehicles (UAVs), commonly known as drones, were used by the U.S. military to attack terrorist hiding spots along the Afghanistan-Pakistan border.

ISAF's *mandate* was initially limited to providing security in and around Kabul. In October 2003, the United Nations Security Council extended ISAF's mandate to cover all of Afghanistan. The mission was expanded in four stages between 2003 and 2006, allowing NATO troops to gradually take over operations from American soldiers.

In addition to providing security, the NATO forces also worked to train an army and police force for Afghanistan, so that the national government could one day stand on its own without requiring international help. NATO also set up teams of workers who helped to rebuild the infrastructure of each province. They built roads and bridges, established schools and medical clinics, and developed sources of fresh water for towns and villages.

With the Taliban and al-Qaeda fighters waging a guerrilla war and launching suicide bombing attacks against U.S. troops as well as government targets in the cities of Afghanistan, the NATO force had to increase their *counterinsurgency* operations in 2006. Afghan and NATO troops would work together to clear insurgents out of a town or village, then they would rebuild it so that the locals would support the national government, rather than the militants.

In 2005, the CIA secretly began a new program that targeted al-Qaeda's leaders around the world. Unmanned aircraft equipped with high-resolution cameras and powerful missiles, called Predator drones, were used to observe areas where terrorists were suspected to be hiding, such as in the region along the border between Afghanistan and northwest Pakistan. The drones could fly up to two miles above a target, so they could spy on suspects without being detected. When a terrorist was identified, the drone could fire its missiles at the enemy.

The drone program succeeded in killing many high-ranking terrorists. The program also forced terrorists to be more careful and restricted their movements. however, it also drew criticism because at times Pakistani

Since 2007, NATO has worked to rebuild the country. (Top) Students of the Nang Abad School near Herat. (Right) NATO workers help to bring fresh water to the village of Baghlan.

A NATO program called the Virtual Silk Highway (SILK) provides high-speed Internet access via satellite to Kabul University and other schools in Afghanistan.

Some of the weapons collected from Afghan fighters in Kabul under a 2008 disarmament program sponsored by the United Nations.

civilians were accidentally killed by drone missile attacks.

Pakistan's government also grew concerned over the number of Taliban fighters who crossed over into Pakistani territory, as these fighters began to destabilize the region. In 2007 and 2008, Pakistan's army began to attack the tribes of the Waziristan region along the border that supported and sheltered the Taliban refugees from Afghanistan.

A Long War Winds Down

In 2009, Afghans re-elected Hamid Karzai as president, despite the many problems with his administration. Karzai had angered U.S. leaders by speaking out against civilian casualties caused by NATO counterinsurgency efforts and drone strikes. Corruption, continued terrorist activities, a floundering economy, and many human rights violations marred Karzai's two terms in office. In 2014, Abdullah Abdullah and Ashraf Ghani were elected to head Afghanistan's government.

In early 2011, American intelligence officials tracked Osama bin Laden to a compound in Abbottabad, Pakistan. On May 2, 2011, U.S. Navy

Members of the Afghan National Army (ANA) meet with a tribal elder in the village of Safidbarah, in western Afghanistan.

ISAF soldiers stand guard over Kabul. Both the United States and NATO ended their combat missions in Afghanistan in December 2014, turning over responsibility for security within the country to the Afghan National Army.

SEALs raided the compound and killed the terrorist leader. Mullah Omar's whereabouts remained unknown, although in 2015 the remnants of the Taliban issued a statement that the reclusive leader was still alive and in charge of their organization.

Although conflict continues, the war began winding down after the death of bin Laden in 2011, as NATO leaders began withdrawing its forces from Afghanistan. At its height, the ISAF included more than 130,000 soldiers from more than 50 countries. Those soldiers were completely withdrawn from Afghanistan by the end of 2014. The U.S. military also ended combat operations that year, leaving just a small force in the country until the end of 2016. In January 2015, NATO launched the new non-combat

Resolute Support Mission to train, advise and assist Afghan security forces and institutions. NATO and its partners are committed to provide financial support to sustain the Afghan forces until the end of 2017.

The War in Afghanistan, lasting from October 2001 to December 2014, was the longest sustained war in the history of the United States. More than 4,000 American or ISAF soldiers have been killed, along with over 15,000 Afghan soldiers. And despite billions of dollars of humanitarian and reconstruction aid from the United States and other donors, Afghanistan remains a land with many problems, including terrorist attacks, poverty, government corruption, a lack of clean water and health care, and an educational system in shambles. But despite these problems, the sacrifices made by U.S. soldiers have created the conditions that may enable Afghans to rise out of their unstable past and create a secure future together.

 ## TEXT-DEPENDENT QUESTIONS

1. What valley did Operation Anaconda attempt to clear of Taliban fighters in 2002?
2. At what conference was the framework for a transitional Afghan government created?
3. What was the purpose of the International Security Assistance Force (ISAF)

 ## RESEARCH PROJECT

Using the Internet, search for stories about the proposed Iraq and Afghanistan Veterans Memorial in Washington, D.C. What groups support the idea of the Iraq and Afghanistan Veterans Memorial? Where would they like it to be located? Are there any suggested plans or designs for the memorial? Write a one-page paper on what you learn, and share it with your class.

Chronology

1978   The Communist People's Democratic Party of Afghanistan (PDPA) leads the Saur Revolution, which overthrows the government of General Muhammad Daoud.

1979   In December, the Soviet Union invades Afghanistan in support of the Communist regime. The international community protests against the Soviet invasion and occupation.

1980   Armed groups known as *mujahideen* begin fighting back against the occupying Soviet force. They receive small amounts of covert aid from the United States, Pakistan, and other countries.

1989   The Soviet Union withdraws its troops from Afghanistan, but continues to provide weapons and financial aid to the Communist government of Mohammad Najibullah.

1992   The Najibullah government collapses, and most of the *mujahideen* groups agree to form a transitional government with Burhanuddin Rabbani as president. Gulbuddin Hekmatyar's Hezb-e Islami group refuses to participate in the new government, and Hekmatyar attempts to capture Kabul. A civil war begins.

1996   The Taliban drives the Rabbani government into exile, takes control of Kabul, and declares the Islamic Emirate of Afghanistan, in which a strict version of Islamic law is enforced. Osama bin Laden is permitted to set up al-Qaeda training camps inside the country.

1998   The United States fires cruise missiles at al-Qaeda camps in Afghanistan in retaliation for bombings at the U.S. embassies in Kenya and Tanzania.

1999   The U.N. imposes sanctions on the Taliban and demands that al-Qaeda leader Osama bin Laden be handed over for trial.

2001　On September 11, al-Qaeda carries out terrorist attacks that destroy the World Trade Center in New York City and damage the Pentagonnear Washington, D.C. On October 7, the United States and Great Britain begin a bombardment of Afghanistan. In December, Hamid Karzai is chosen as head of an interim government. Bin Laden escapes to Pakistan during the Battle of Tora Bora.

2003　In August, NATO takes control over the International Security Assistance Force (ISAF).

2004　In January a loya jirga adopts a new constitution; Hamid Karzai is elected president in Afghanistan's first democratic election, held in October.

2005　Parliamentary elections are held in September, and the Parliament meets for the first time in 30 years.

2006　NATO assumes responsibility for security across Afghanistan, taking command in the east from a US-led coalition force.

2008　President Karzai accuses Afghan and US-led forces of killing at least 89 civilians in an air strike in the province of Herat.

2009　President Karzai is re-elected after an election that is plagued by Taliban attacks and claims of fraud. U.S. President Obama increases U.S. troop numbers in Afghanistan to 100,000.

2010　In February, NATO forces begin a major operation to secure Helmand province. Parliamentary elections are disrupted by Taliban attacks and the results are long-delayed and their validity questioned. At a summit in Lisbon in November, NATO agrees on a plan to transfer control to Afghan security forces by 2014.

2011　In January, President Karzai makes the first official visit of an Afghan leader to Russia since the Soviet occupation. The Taliban breach a prison in Kandahar and 500 prisoners escape. Kandahar governor Ahmad Wali Karzai and former president Burhanuddin Rabbani are assassinated. A loya jirga approves Karzai's plan for a 10-year military partnership with the U.S. On May 2, U.S. special forces raid a private compound in Abbottabad, Pakistan, and kill al-Qaeda founder Osama bin Laden.

2012 The U.S. suspends training for Afghan police to investigate attacks on foreign troops by apparent Afghan police and soldiers.

2013 In June, NATO forces transfer command of all military operations to the Afghan army.

2014 The worst Taliban attack on foreign civilians since 2001 kills 13 people in Kabul. In October, the U.S. and Britain end combat operations in Afghanistan.

2015 NATO begins new mission of training and supporting Afghan security forces called "Resolute Support." Taliban representatives and Afghan leaders hold informal peace talks in Qatar.

Further Reading

Bolger, Daniel. *Why We Lost: A General's Inside Account of the Iraq and Afghanistan Wars*. New York: Houghton Mifflin, 2014.

Chayes, Sarah. *The Punishment of Virtue: Inside Afghanistan After the Taliban*. New York: The Penguin Press, 2006.

Fairweather, Jack. *The Good War: Why We Couldn't Win the War or the Peace in Afghanistan*. New York: Basic Books, 2014.

Jones, Seth G. *In the Graveyard of Empires: America's War in Afghanistan*. New York: W.W. Norton, 2010.

Kallen, Stuart A. *The War In Afghanistan*. Minneapolis: ReferencePoint Press, 2013.

Rashid, Ahmed. *Descent into Chaos: The U.S. and the Disaster in Pakistan, Afghanistan, and Central Asia*. New York: Viking, 2009.

Internet Resources

http://www.defense.gov

The website of the U.S. Department of Defense provides information about military activities in Afghanistan and other parts of the world.

http://www.state.gov/p/sca/ci/af

The U.S. State Department website has a thorough section on the background of Afghanistan, including its economics, politics, and other information.

https://www.cia.gov/library/publications/the-world-factbook/geos/af.html

The CIA World Factbook website provides a great deal of statistical information about Afghanistan and its people. It is regularly updated.

www.mideasti.org

An extensive resource geared to educate Americans about the Middle East. This academic site includes loads of information for research.

www.un.org/english

The English-language web page for the United Nations can be searched for Afghanistan-related stories and information.

Index

Abdullah, Abdullah, 55
Afghanistan
    and the Taliban, 11–12 27–32, 33–44,
        45–51, 52, 55, 57
    Soviet occupation of, 11, *13*, 14,
        18–22, 23, 24, 30, 39
    ethic groups in, 13–14, 31
    geography and terrain of, 14, 15, 34,
        35, *36*, 37, *43*, 46, 47
    government of, 16, 18, 22, 23–24,
        27–30, 33–34, 40, 48, 50–51, 55
    civil war in, 23–32
Afghan Interim Authority, 48
Afghan National Army (ANA), 55
Ali, Hazrat, 42–43
Alma Tak Mountains, 35
Amin, Hafizullah, 18, 19

Baghlan, *53*
Bagram, *36*, 37
Bamiyan, *29*, 30
Bonn Conference, 40, 48, 50
Boston, 7
Bush, George W., *11*, 12, 33

Camp Rhino, 39
Carter, Jimmy, 20
Central Intelligence Agency (CIA), 21 43,
    52
Cheney, Richard "Dick," *11*
Cold War, 15, 20

Daoud, Muhammad, 15, 18
Deobandi tradition, 11, 27
Directorate for Inter–Services Intelligence
    (ISI), 21, 27
Dostum, Abdul Rashid, 23, 31, 34, 36, 37,
    38, 50
Doud, Mohammed, 35, 38
drone attacks, 52

ethnic groups
    Pashtun, 13–14, 15, 24, 30, 40, 47
    Tajik, 14, 31, *35*, 51
    Uzbek, 14, 23, 31, *34*, 50
    Turkmen, 14, 31
    Hazara, 14, 31

Fahim, Mohammed, 35, 37
France, 17, *51*
Franks, Tommy, 43

Gardez, 47
Germany, 17
Ghani, Ashraf, 55
Ghazni, 29
Gorbachev, Mikhail, 22
Great Britain, 17, 33, 34, 48

ul–Haq, Zia, 21
Hekmatyar, Gulbuddin, 24, 25, 27
Herat, 14, 27, *53*
Hezb–e Islami, 24, 27

India, 11, 13
International Security Assistance Force
    (ISAF), 51
Iran, 13, 18, 20, 27
Islamism, 11–12, 16–18

Jalalabad, 27, 42

Kabul, 15, *16*, *17*, 19, 23, 25, 27, 29, *35*,
    36, 37, 44, 52, *54*, *56*
Kabul University, *54*
Kandahar Province, 27, *36*, 37, 39,
    40–42, 44, 51
Kapisa Province, *51*
Karmal, Babrak, 19, 22
Karshi Kandabad, 34
Karzai, Hamid, 40, 41, 48, 50, 51, 55
Kazakh SSR, 19

Numbers in **bold italics** refer to captions.

Kenya, 30
Khomeini, Ayatollah Ruhollah, 19, 20
Kirgiz SSR, 19
Kondoz, *36,* 38

bin Laden, Osama, 11, *30*, 31, 44, 55–56
Los Angeles, 9
loya jirga, 18, 50

Mazar–e Sharif, *26*, 35, *36*, 37, *38*
Massood, Ahmad Shah, 24, *26*, 31, 32, 35, 37, 51
Moscow, 18
Muhammad (Prophet), 17
mujahideen, 19–22, 23–25, *26,* 30, 40
Muslim Brotherhood, 18

Najibullah, Muhammad, 22, 23, 24
The Netherlands, 17
New York City, 7, 8, 9
North Atlantic Treaty Organization (NATO), 51, 52, *53*
Northern Alliance, *26*, 30–32, 34–38, *39*

Omar, Muhammad, 27, 34, 56
Operation Anaconda, 47

Pakistan, 11, 18, *19*, 20, 22, 24, 27, 31, 43, 48, 51, 52
Paktia Province, 47
Panjshir Valley, 24, 37
Pentagon, 8, 10, 39, 48
People's Democratic Party of Afghanistan (PDPA), 18, 19
Peshawar, 21
Peshawar Accord, 24
Portugal, 17

al-Qaeda, 10–11, 30, 32, 33, 34, *36*, 37, 42–44, 45–51, 52–57
Qanuni, Yunus, 50

Rabbani, Burhanuddin, 27, 31
Reagan, Ronald, 20
Rumsfeld, Donald H., *11, 35, 44*

Safidbarah, 55

Saudi Arabia, 21, 24, 27, 30
Saur Revolution, 18
Sayd Alim Kalay, 41
September 11 attack, 7–10, *11*, 12, 32, 33
Shahi Kowt Valley, 47
Shamali Plains, 37
Shanksville, 8
Sharzai, Gul, 41
Singesar, 27
Soviet Union, 15–16, 18–22, 24, 30, 34

Tajik SSR, 19
Takur Ghar, 47
Taliban, 11, 12, 27–32, 33–44, 45–51, 52, 55, 57
Taloqan, *36*, 38
Tanzania, 30
Taraki, Nur Muhammad, 18
Tarin Kowt, 40
Tora Bora, *33*, *36*, 42–44, 46
Transitional State of Afghanistan, 50

United Arab Emirates, 27
United Nations, 20, 30, 52, *54*
United States, 15, 20, 30, 33–44, 45–57
U.S. Capitol, 9
unmanned aerial vehicle (UAV). *See* drone attacks
Uzbekistan, 34, 39

Virginia, 8
Virtual Silk Highway, *54*

Washington, D.C., 8
Waziristan, 55
White House, 8, 9
Wilson, Charlie, 21
World Trade Center, 8, 9, 10

Zahir Shah (king), 15
Zormat, 47

SERIES GLOSSARY

blockade—an effort to cut off supplies, war material, or communications by a particular area, by force or the threat of force.

guerrilla warfare—a type of warfare in which a small group of combatants, such as armed civilians, use hit-and-run tactics to fight a larger and less mobile traditional army. The purpose is to weaken an enemy's strength through small skirmishes, rather than fighting pitched battles where the guerrillas would be at a disadvantage.

intelligence—the analysis of information collected from various sources in order to provide guidance and direction to military commanders.

logistics—the planning and execution of movements by military forces, and the supply of those forces.

salient—a pocket or bulge in a fortified line or battle line that projects into enemy territory.

siege—a military blockade of a city or fortress, with the intent of conquering it at a later stage.

tactics—the science and art of organizing a military force, and the techniques for using military units and their weapons to defeat an enemy in battle.